THE BLACK TAIL OF CHAN

A Very Special Cat

by Chan

The Black Tail of Chan – A Very Special Cat
Copyright © 2015 Chris and Ann Dunn
All rights reserved

ISBN-10: 0-9930879-5-7
ISBN-13: 978-0-9930879-5-0

Published by Hawkesbury Press 2015
Hawkesbury Upton, Gloucestershire GL9 1AS, England
No parts of this publication may be reproduced, stored in a retrieval system, or transmitted in any form or by any means, electronic, mechanical, photocopying, recording, or otherwise, without the prior written permission of the copyright holder.

This book is sold subject to the condition that it shall not, by way of trade or otherwise, be lent, resold, hired out, or otherwise circulated without the publisher's prior consent in any form of binding or cover other than that in which it is published and without a similar condition, including this condition, being imposed on any subsequent purchaser. Under no circumstances may any part of this book be photocopied for resale.

Cover photography by Dr Chris Dunn
Cover design by Debbie Young
Interior design by Debbie Young

In fond memory of a very special cat
CHAN
(CH = Chris, AN = Ann)
1990 – 29 November 2007

This little book was written
as a lasting tribute
to a much-loved pet cat, Chan,
who enjoyed 18 happy years
as the special friend of
Chris and Ann Dunn
in a small Gloucestershire village

It describes Chan's life
as he might have told it himself

My First Meeting with Dad and Mum

From the day we met, I called them Dad and Mum, and that's how I thought of them too. You see, I'd never known my real parents.

Apparently when I was still very small, I was picked up wandering the streets of Gloucester, put into a cage, and carted off in some vehicle to a place where there were lots of other cats (and dogs).

One day, one of the helpers at this place took me out of my cage, and I made a real fuss of her, purring and trying to roll onto my back along her arm.

Then Dad and Mum were there, tickling my chin and generally making a fuss of me. Boy, did they seem keen! Somehow I knew straight away that we were going to be very happy together.

But then they were gone.

Going to my New Home

The next thing I remember is waking up with some tenderness around my groin and a general feeling that something was missing.

But what joy! Who should appear again but Dad and Mum? This time they were carrying some sort of cage.

Pleased as I was to see them, my enjoyment was tempered when they brusquely put me into the cage with another cat. This little tortoiseshell creature was quite sweet, but didn't really smell all there. It seemed she was coming with us.

Again we were put into a vehicle, much quieter than the one I had experienced before, but neither my companion nor I were very comfortable. We were cramped in that cage and were kept being tossed about.

We weren't in there for long before Dad pulled the car up a steep but short road. We stopped moving, and everything went quiet, except for us.

Halfway House

Dad carried our cage out and put it on the floor of a dismal building that smelt vaguely of another cat. It was cold and bare, but when he opened the cage door, we were free! Well, sort of free.

There was a little door in a much bigger door, which Dad and Mum went through, into what we later learnt was the house. A second small door led through another large door into what we discovered was the garden. But we couldn't open any of these doors.

So we explored and sniffed around the room. Dad and Mum brought us some meat and some milk. I wasn't very keen on the meat, and I never did develop a taste for milk, particularly the stuff without any fat in it, even though we cats are supposed to love it.

Settling In

Days went by for me and Charlie, as I learnt to think of her, because that was what Dad and Mum called her.

While we lived in this building, we were fed twice a day, and had a big fuss each time we were fed, but we didn't see much of Dad or Mum.

We couldn't even get out, although we could clamber over things and look out of the window. We found some old material that we made into a rough bed, but it could still be cold.

And, horror of horrors, we had to relieve ourselves on some sort of grey gravel. If Charlie used it first, I ended up standing in her mess to do my business. I always tried to get to the gravel first every morning, straight after it had been changed.

Open House

As the days wore on, we were eventually allowed into the house. It was wonderful!

There were nice comfortable chairs on which to curl up next to things on the wall that were often hot, at least in the mornings and evenings.

Sometimes we chose to make a mess in this lovely warm environment. That didn't go down well with Dad and Mum, and we were hastily picked up and dumped on the grey gravel in the room in which we still spent most of our time.

But what fun we had in the house, and how warm and comfortable it felt, particularly when we thought back to our experience before the ride in the cage.

Exploring the Garden

After a few days, when Dad and Mum were at home, they took us into the garden, where we were allowed to wander around.

Dad in particular seemed quite nervous about this. He never let us jump up onto the fence, from which we would be able to see the world.

At first, they only let us out after they'd smeared some lovely yellow stuff on our paws, and only ever when we were hungry.

Our Stylish New Look

We soon settled in well. Dad and Mum were ever so kind, even though they were always trying to stop us going too far. They even put collars around our necks with little bells on that always seemed to jingle if we got anywhere close to one of those things with feathers, of which there were plenty in the garden!

Our collars also had little round metal things with our names on, and Dad's and Mum's, in case we got lost – as if we would!

Free at Last

Then one day, glory be, we were let loose – really loose, into the garden, coming and going as we pleased through the little door, which we opened ourselves with a clatter. (We still weren't allowed into the house without supervision, though.)

We didn't go far – we didn't want to – but we roamed the garden and visited our neighbour. He was a Mr McGregor type: often smoking, and nearly always working away in one of his greenhouses. At various times when we lived next to him and his family, he had a dog or a cat. While we generally tried to keep out of the way of the dog, both he and the cat were friendly.

My Greenhouse Adventure

One day, I decided to see what Mr McGregor was up to with all his plants by looking over his shoulder. This was not so easy when I was only half a metre tall, and he was sitting on a stool three times as high.

So I thought I'd get up onto the roof of his greenhouse and look down on him from there. Another of my big mistakes!

Claws are fine for rough surfaces like trees and fences, and to scratch on furniture (oops!), but not so good on solid, slippery surfaces like glass.

As I landed heavily from my perch, my front right paw went through the glass. I limped back home with red stuff running all down my leg. Dad held me tight while he washed my foot. It was so demeaning, and in front of Charlie as well! Didn't he know I could have done it just as well myself?

Our First Winter

As our first winter with Dad and Mum came on, it really was cold in our room, so they allowed us to spend more and more time in their house. What fun! One of my favourite games was chasing Charlie up and down the stairs. This was especially fun because neither of us were really supposed to go upstairs.

I loved to run up and down the curtains too. Going up was fine, but it was always a bit of a challenge getting back down again without either knocking something over or landing awkwardly. Who said cats always land on their feet? Even if we do, it can sometimes hurt if we don't land all square on our four paws.

A Close Shave

Looking back, I think I always was a bit of a mischief, frequently getting into all sorts of trouble.

One day, probably a Sunday, I was determined to find out where the lovely smell was coming from and how close I could get to it, particularly because everything seemed beautifully warm around this smell. When Mum wasn't looking, I leapt up onto the cupboards and started strolling around.

Ouch! What was that not-so-nice smell? Mum dashed to the rescue, brushing my face.

I wondered why I felt a little lopsided until I got a glimpse of my reflection: long white whiskers on one side of my face, but where were the whiskers on the other? Gone! Singed off! Of course, they soon grew back, but I never ever walked across the top of that hot metal cupboard again, even when there were scrump-delicious smells coming from it!

Snack Time

Charlie and I were never short of food, but hey, cats are cats, and we hunt birds and mice, don't we? How could either of us ignore our instincts?

Quite frequently, we would bring in little presents for Dad and Mum. It was funny how they never seemed to appreciate these gifts. They always tried to catch them (Dad once got bitten for his efforts) and put them back outside, only for us to go out, catch them again, and bring them right back.

But that wasn't much fun really, and we soon got fed up with it, although I suspect it was rather more 'me' than 'we' doing most of the catching!

Tough Guy

I don't know why, but I somehow got a reputation for being rather short-tempered. Some even thought of me as a bit of a thug. I really wasn't.

I just didn't like being played with, particularly by children, who never seemed to know when I'd had enough. So I lashed out very occasionally, but, as far as I can remember, I only twice caught someone other than Dad: first, the little girl next door, and then, many years later, Dad's granddaughter who had come to stay. Mum made a big fuss of the latter, even though I had hardly broken her skin. Still, the fuss stopped the little girl from crying, so I guess that was good, even if she did keep well away from me during the rest of her stay.

Taking the Tablets

Although Dad let me get away with lots of misdemeanours, he always handled me a lot. He could be quite firm when he needed to do something like give me tablets.

I usually gave in, knowing he was bigger and stronger than me, so was likely to win in the end. Charlie always fought him, and sometimes scratched him quite badly, even when she had been wrapped up tightly. Yet I was considered the thug and she to be a quiet, demure little thing! Sometimes life just isn't fair.

As I got older and needed medicine more often, I would sit placidly between Dad's legs as he knelt on the floor, opening my mouth with one hand, and sliding a tablet into my throat with the other. This was seldom comfortable, but he and Mum were always so kind that I knew they wouldn't do it if it wasn't to make me feel better.

My Pet Hates #1

There were two things I never ever got used to, and the first of these was annoying noises.

At least while I could still hear, the rattle and rustle of the shiny aluminium foil that Mum used to wrap things in – somehow that noise went all through my body. At the first sight of the roll, I was up and out of the room until peace and quiet returned.

Fireworks or thunder were different matters. Dad tried to keep me in when fireworks were going off, but as I grew and became stronger, I would rush at my little door. Once the door flew open, I found shelter from the noise outside in my own way.

After that, Dad and Mum just left me to come and go during fireworks or thunder.

My Pet Hates #2

The second thing I never got used to was being brushed and combed. My long white fur often got knotted, despite my best efforts, so I suppose it was inevitable that Dad would try to help clear the tangles.

I could put up with being brushed for a little while, particularly if it was just on my back, but I got very cross once the brush or comb went anywhere near my belly or tail. Then I'd try to warn Dad I'd had enough.

I wasn't backwards in coming forwards to let everyone know how I felt. I'd thrash my tail about and even go for Dad's ankles if he didn't stop, as he soon learnt to!

My Turkish Van Heritage

Dad and Mum thought I was partly a Turkish Van cat, a type of cat that is supposed to like water, but I never did enjoy a bath whenever I came into the house covered in mud.

And I really didn't want to join Mum in the bath one time! I was just exploring the ledge around the bath – aren't cats supposed to be curious? – and simply lost my footing. Then of course I had to rely on Mum to lift me out, because I couldn't get a grip on all that shiny surface.

When I was much older and had lots of knots in the long hair around my abdomen in which fleas seemed to thrive, I knew Dad was just doing his best for me when he put me in the bath. I'd let him hold my front legs up so I was just about standing in knee-high water while he combed and scrubbed my tum, but all the same, how ignominious for a cat like me!

Getting into Scrapes

Looking back on my youth, I got into my share of mischief, and sometimes that seemed to focus around roofs.

Not only was there the occasion of Mr McGregor's glasshouse, but I also managed to get stuck – or so everyone thought – on the roof of our other neighbour's house.

Dad's ladders couldn't reach, and he was obviously getting concerned, as were the neighbours who turned out to watch. So, after making a point, I consented to come down gracefully on a sloping bit of roof, from where Dad could reach me and lift me down by the scruff of my neck. What a cheek!

A Tragic Accident

The only thing that I am ashamed of happened one weekend when Dad and Mum had gone away. Mrs McGregor was feeding Charlie and me – Mum always arranged for someone to feed us in our own home when they went away rather than putting us in a cattery.

Charlie and I were having our usual bit of rough stuff, chasing one another all over the house, when she charged out through our little doors, closely followed by me. Through the garage and down the path we went, straight out onto the road.

Charlie didn't have a chance. She was hit hard by a fast-moving car that didn't stop, and was thrown onto the pavement quite dead. I went up to her, gave her a little lick and told her how sorry I was. We chased one another a lot, and, although she did chase me sometimes, I'm afraid it was usually me doing the chasing.

I guess Mr McGregor must have buried Charlie, as she wasn't on the side of the road for long. I slunk back into the house, feeling low and guilty.

Road Safety

Sometimes things seem to go in circles. Even after Charlie was killed, I continued to explore the houses and gardens opposite ours, crossing the road without any thought.

It must have been late afternoon or early evening when I went off on another of these adventures, as it was getting dark and Dad had just come in from work. I remember a squeal and then a thump on the side of my head.

Next thing I knew, I woke up being cuddled in the arms of a clearly upset Dad. I must have been knocked unconscious because I felt very groggy for some hours and retained a bruise – a blue-black mark on an otherwise white ear – for the rest of my life.

After that adventure, I was much less likely to cross the road. If I really needed to, I'd sit down to listen for any cars, only crossing the road when I could hear nothing coming.

Moving House

I never really did get used to riding in cars. Dad and Mum would put me in, then let me wander around and finally settle down, after much shouting on my part. At least it was better than being forced into some sort of carrying case.

One day, various people were coming and going. My favourite chair and bed were moved and put into a large van. Finally, Dad and Mum put me in the car.

We seemed to drive around for hours before we pulled up outside a strange building. The engine was switched off, and Dad carried me into our new house.

New and strange it may have been, but the whole atmosphere seemed vaguely the same. Unfortunately, none of the doors had flaps for me to go out, and I was kept in for what seemed like ages. I even had to use a tray with that grey grit in again.

Home from Home

When I was eventually let out, it was a bit like when Dad and Mum took me to our first home. I was allowed out, but not for long. Just as I was thinking I might like to explore over the fence or down the path at the back of the house, they'd grab me and bring me back inside.

Although everything was very different – house, garden, neighbouring garden, and a much quieter road out the front – it somehow seemed the same.

It's difficult to explain. Although I had never been in this house or road before, it seemed the same as the previous house – and it was, almost!

Dad soon fixed my own doors into the back ones of the new house, and I was allowed to come and go as I pleased again.

Fresh Start

Soon I went exploring, walking through all sorts of gardens and paths, very carefully crossing a quiet road.

Eventually I found our old home, and I even said hello to Mrs McGregor. It seemed we weren't far from where we had been living before.

Dad and Mum had just tried to confuse me by driving for what seemed like hours from our old house to the new one, yet I'd walked back to it in no time. Don't people know we cats have a homing instinct?

Soon I decided I much preferred our new house. After all, that was where Dad and Mum were now living, and I definitely wanted to be with them.

Hunting

We soon settled into a new routine. I divided my time between the house in the winter months, usually managing to find a warm spot by a radiator, and the garden during the summer, where I either stretched out on a stone table in the sun or sheltered under some plants when things got too warm.

I roamed all over the gardens either side of us, although I had to look out for two large dogs belonging to one neighbour.

There were always birds and mice to catch. Funny, Dad never did appreciate the presents I brought in. Certainly, I didn't catch them because I was hungry.

Feeding

Dad and Mum fed me very well, finally settling on the foods I would eat most of the time. At least twice a day there were special treats, such as prawns (yum yum!) which Dad used to feed me one by one. I liked them so much, I think Dad was concerned he might lose his fingers each time he gave me one.

I always greeted Dad and Mum warmly when they returned home in the evenings, and they always made a fuss of me.

A New Feline Friend

One day, the neighbour with the dogs acquired a cat not unlike Charlie. I decided to be friends with Dinah (for that was her name) on my own terms – at least in my house.

At the back of our house was a conservatory with a flat plastic roof, hung inside with sailcloth blinds, presumably to keep out some of the summer heat. By climbing up onto a refrigerator then a cupboard, I could get into these blinds, which made very comfortable hammocks. Although rather hot in summer, the one over the radiator was a delight in winter.

In my new-found fondness for Dinah, I invited her to share a hammock with me, although she needed a little persuading to make the climb. I even let her share my food, especially anything I didn't particularly like.

Eventually the neighbour sold up and moved, but Dinah stayed with the neighbour on the other side of our house.

The New Mr McGregor

The neighbour was another Mr McGregor type. He was extremely kind, and he took over Dad's feeding duties when Dad and Mum were away.

I can assure you, there is absolutely no truth to the rumour that one day, many years later, I got into his kitchen through the window that Dinah used, curled up on his table, and pretended to be angry when he tried to turn me out into the cold. Would I have done that?

Pedigree Friends

I also learnt to like very much the neighbours across the road. They lived in a big house with a large garden, and they also had a cat.

Because theirs was an old house, there always seemed to be plenty of ways to get inside, particularly if it was cold outside. This became a sort of second home for me, although I used it only irregularly.

When they moved away, some new people arrived with two very superior-looking pedigree cats. I never had much to do with them, but I found their delicious biscuits irresistible. I'd sneak across the road once or twice a day and have a snack – or two, or three, or four. Not as good as prawns, but lovely nevertheless.

I think the neighbours might have complained to Dad and Mum, because very soon these biscuits started appearing in my own dishes. I tended to prefer meat sometimes and biscuits at other times – but prawns always!

Visiting the Vet

Life went on and it was good.

I suppose I must have occasionally gone to see the animal doctor, whom Dad called Nick or the vet, but generally I was in good health, and I lived life to the full.

Once I developed a lump on my right shoulder – did Dad call it a sebaceous cyst? – but it didn't really bother me, and I just learnt to live with it.

The Ship's Cat

Dad and Mum started to take me on what they called a boat – a long, narrow thing with water all round it.

It had a large bed right next to a pipe that was always warm, and a coal fire that heated up a radiator. Dad and Mum were always there, so everything was okay.

The first few times I went to the boat, everyone just sat around talking, and it was all very quiet. Then we used to stay overnight, and soon we were going off in this thing for weeks on end.

I had the run of the boat, but I was very seldom allowed to leave it. I suppose Dad thought I'd go off somewhere and not return. I don't think I would have done that, but I suppose I might have got lost and not found my way back to wherever they were moored.

On the Move

Dad always closed the back door of the boat when we were moving so that I couldn't get out and look around. When he finally realised I wasn't going to go anywhere, I was sometimes allowed to sit at his feet. It was okay down there, peering round the side, but I didn't much like it when he put me up on the roof in the wind, even though I did get a better view.

Sometimes we saw other boats with dogs on them, but only very occasionally with a cat. Generally when people on other boats saw me, I was the centre of attention.

The worst part of not being allowed off was that I had to use a tray again, but I insisted it was in Dad's bathroom next to the warm radiator, and not out in the cold engine room at the back of the boat. With three of us in or on the bed at night, it could get a bit crowded!

Mutiny

After one long trip, I decided I wanted to stay on the boat. I wasn't being awkward, I'd just got used to things. So after Dad had chased me around for a while, I curled up under the bed in the most difficult places for Dad to reach me. He had several attempts, and I'm afraid I lashed out at him every time. Then he came at me with a towel, threw it over me, and bundled me out of the boat and into the car.

I was horrified when I saw the state of his arms. How badly I must have scratched him. There seemed to be blood everywhere!

Poor Dad. I'm sure he knew I didn't really mean it, and that it was just my frustration at having been cooped up on the boat for so long. I never ever did anything that bad to anyone again. Instead I thrashed my big black bushy tail around to warn them how upset I was becoming.

All Quiet

On one of the boat trips, I realised that although I could feel the boat moving, I could no longer hear the chug-chug of the engine. While I could see aluminium foil being used, I couldn't hear its annoying rustle.

I was taken off to the vet. After much clapping of hands, that I saw but didn't hear, and poking and prodding around my ears, everyone decided I was deaf.

Now, rather than listening to work out where Dad and Mum were, I had to make myself heard so they could come and find (and feed) me. Boy, did I manage to make some impressive noises! How effective they were too: a couple of good howls, and Dad or Mum were immediately by my side at the refrigerator getting me food, or sometimes just picking me up for a cuddle to make sure it was only a 'Where are you?' howl, not an 'I'm hurting' one.

Another Trip to the Vet

We've jumped ahead a few years. The visit to the vet about my deafness was the second of my more serious, less routine trips.

The first time was over a weekend when I really did start to feel very poorly. I ached all over, and I wanted to be sick, but couldn't because I wasn't eating. At the same time I was making a real mess around the garden, or at least on the bit of garden closest to the house.

Dad and Mum were obviously very concerned. Although it was a Sunday, they must have contacted the vet, because pretty soon I was in the car, and then we were at the clinic.

Dad and Mum left me in the hands of some lovely people who made a big fuss of me. They attached me to some sort of tube that went into the back of one of my front paws.

On the Mend

Slowly I started to feel better. Dad came in one day to visit me, and I couldn't believe how wonderful it was to see him. When I tried to get out of the cage into his arms, he looked very relieved that I was so keen.

But, disappointingly, I was put back in the cage. It was another couple of days before I saw Dad again, and this time he took me home.

After that event, trips to the vet became more regular and frequent. At least once a year I was weighed, had cold metal things placed all over my body, hard bits of food flicked off my teeth, something stuck up my bottom (how very degrading!), and the odd needle or two poked into the back of my neck.

A Nose Job

The next trip to the vet was for a snotty nose. Actually, I think I just got some food stuck up one nostril. Uncle Nick poked and prodded it, and I heard him say something about putting me to sleep to have a closer look and to extract whatever was causing the problem.

Dad clearly didn't like that idea, so it was a case of more needles before being sent home to a course of tablets.

I really didn't like being given these things, even though they were fairly small. Dad ended up being very good at getting them down my throat without hurting me or letting me taste them. I still didn't enjoy the experience, but it was better than more needles. Besides, I trusted him to do only what he thought was best for me.

We had several sessions of snotty nose, needles, and tablets, and I'm not sure Uncle Nick ever found out what the problem was.

The Disappearing Dad

There was a time when Dad disappeared for weeks on end, which seemed to be something to do with his job.

Mum would also vanish on alternate weekends, when I assumed she had flown off to visit him. He had gone to work in Norway, where Mum's son lives.

Thanks to them and Mr McGregor, I always had food, biscuits, and water, and a warm house to return to from my foraging trips to various gardens.

I realised very early on when Mum or Dad were away, because Mr McGregor always fed me fresh chicken. I never did find out why he did that. Maybe he was unable to open my usual tinned food, or didn't like the smell of it. Sometimes I didn't find it very appealing either.

I was always pleased when Mum returned, and especially when Dad reappeared, although I tried not to show it too much as I wanted to maintain some level of indifference, independence, and superiority.

A Contented Cat

The years rolled on, and life was good. I had a loving dad and mum who made sure I had all the food I wanted, and who frequently treated me to my favourite: prawns.

There was always somewhere warm in the house, even when Dad and Mum were out or had gone off for a few days.

Generally, they were around, and whenever they did go off on the boat, they took me with them. I was quite happy, despite being largely restricted to the boat, except for one weekend when I was allowed off to roam around.

I certainly preferred being with Dad and Mum to being left at home, even when fed regularly by kind Mr McGregor.

Games with Dad

Dad and I developed a special cuddle routine. It started one day when I stretched up his trouser leg. Even though I was only stretching, he put his hands under my front paws and lifted me up to hold me like a human baby on his arm. My front paws were on his shoulder while he rubbed and tickled my ears and chin. Bliss!

Sometimes, I'd roll over and lie along his arm. I had complete confidence that he wouldn't drop me. This trick developed to the extent that when he came into the room and slapped his legs, I'd stretch up them and he'd pick me up for cuddles. Wonderful!

To be honest, some of the attention I bestowed on him might have been cupboard love, fuelled by my desire for special titbits. Even so, I repaid Dad and Mum amply, giving them someone with whom they could share their obvious affection. It really was a wonderful give-and-take arrangement, and I don't think for one minute that Dad and Mum minded.

The Flea Bath

One summer, I seemed to have more than my fair share of livestock. Various powders, collars, and liquids didn't get rid of them.

I also had lots of knots in the long hair on my belly. Here fleas could hide from the insecticides Dad used to try to make life more comfortable for me, and for him and Mum.

One day, he picked me up and gently placed me in warm water up to my armpits. I tried just once to get out of the very same bath that I'd fallen into years before, but Dad was his usual firm self when something had to be done, and I had the confidence in him to let him think he was boss.

I even helped him by putting my front paws on one of his hands and standing on my back legs while he combed and scrubbed my belly. It was very degrading, but I'm sure it was all in a good cause.

Dignity Restored

The water ran away, and I thought that was the end of it, but no. More water came in, and I was thoroughly drenched.

Then Dad lifted me out, put a towel over me, and attempted to rub me dry, but I just ran off to find a place in the house where the sun was shining warmly through a window. I did my own drying down.

I didn't like this bath at the time, but I came out of it cleaner and much more comfortable – and, for the first time in years, almost knot-free.

It's said Turkish Van cats like water. Perhaps, but everything is relative.

Out with the Old Kitchen

The next upheaval in my life was when some men came in to pull down all the kitchen cupboards and throw them outside. They even took down the ceiling.

I treated these chaps with my usual suspicion of newcomers. I kept out of their way, rarely letting them come close, even when all they wanted to do was to make a fuss of me.

There was dust everywhere. Although I couldn't hear anything, I could sense their drills and grinders from the vibration, and it must have been terribly noisy. This work lasted for weeks, and to my annoyance, furniture was rearranged so I couldn't get into my hammocks. I was also unable to get from my door from the outside world into the rest of the house without going through this area of dust, dirt, and noise.

In with the New

While this work was going on, I had to find new places in which to curl up. Several opportunities developed as sheets were placed over various cupboards and carpets. These made cosy little havens for this elderly gentleman cat.

Between you and me, these sheets weren't always as clean and sweet-smelling as they might have been. Very occasionally, they saved me the trouble of having to go out in the cold and rain to relieve myself, but only *very* occasionally!

When all the fuss seemed to be over, I strolled into the new kitchen. Lo and behold, the new stone tiles on the floor were warm. Dad and Mum had installed underfloor heating. More bliss!

I managed to pull down a kitchen cloth onto that lovely, warm floor and it became my bed, conveniently close to where all the food was prepared. I think I might have been in Mum's way once or twice.

Painting and Decorating

If the new kitchen wasn't enough disruption, a couple of weeks later Dad and Mum started moving furniture around again.

Then a stranger came in every day for a week, armed with paintbrushes and other decorating equipment not just for one room, but for two, either side of my new, warm kitchen.

I didn't like him any more than the other fellows, but although he made plenty of dust, at least he wasn't as noisy – and he had more sheets.

Autumn Days

As the days started getting shorter and colder, I went out less and less.

On occasions, Dad had to take me outside when I started scrabbling at the carpet. He even had to stay with me to convince me that I should relieve myself in the garden, not on the dining room carpet.

Helping with Maths

It turned out that Mum taught maths to pupils up to GCSE level, and I was often the topic of questions she posed to the students. Apparently the questions were mainly about Pythagoras's theorem, trigonometry, and loci questions involving mice, birds, and dogs. They were usually about how far I would have to go to find the most direct way from my door to a favourite hunting spot while avoiding dogs. It was something to do with triangles, I was told. Of course, I was always willing to help out, and I impressed the students with my ability.

Lucky Me

Not only was I a maths wizard, but it seems I was also a good luck charm. Because I was famous and all the pupils knew about me, Mum got hold of a photograph of me and made it into little 'Good Luck' cards for the pupils as they got ready to sit their exams. I'm sure with all my talons – oops, I mean talents – they would all have sailed through! Mum gave me a glamorous background: supposedly I was a direct descendent of Queen Cleopatra's cat, whose hooked tail used to keep her rings safe while she bathed.

The Beginning of the End

One Thursday, in the run-up to Christmas, Dad and Mum were later home than usual, and I was hungry. It had been raining all day, and for the first time in a few days I actually had an appetite. I ate some of the meat Dad put down for me, then I had a treat of a few cheesy *Doritos* and some lovely cuddles.

But my left back leg didn't feel right, and I couldn't get comfortable, even on the warm kitchen floor. Dad stroked me a few times and seemed a little concerned, but I wasn't really in any great discomfort.

Dad and Mum had just gone off into another room with trays of their food when suddenly my left leg became unbearably painful. I staggered into the dining room, threw up, and messed on the carpet. Then I started to howl, really howl. This wasn't my 'Where are you, Dad? I'm hungry and want food and cuddles' howl. This was my 'I'm in awful pain, Dad' howl.

Seeking Comfort

Dad came out, made a fuss, and saw I clearly wasn't well. He cleaned up the mess, then tried to hold me. My leg was now so painful that I couldn't move. All I could do was to drag it along behind me as I fell about, trying to find a position in which I could get comfortable and warm without my leg hurting.

Dad carried me upstairs and put me on my blanket on a windowsill over a lovely warm radiator. It was what I wanted, but the pain didn't stop. My leg was swelling around the knee, and I couldn't move it.

Dad lifted me down, and I scrabbled into a box of paper and peed. I couldn't help it. Neither Dad nor Mum were cross, but both were clearly very concerned.

There followed much use of the telephone while I somehow got into the airing cupboard, seeking warmth and gaining some comfort, but not for long.

A Dash to the Vet

Ever so gently, Dad picked me up and placed me in Mum's lap in the car, then he drove, trying unsuccessfully to comfort me at the same time.

We travelled for a while, then I waited in the car before he carried me indoors and placed me on the vet's stainless steel table.

Dad helped while Uncle Nick moved me around, poking and prodding. Mum was in tears as I continued to howl, and it was clear from Dad's breaking voice that he was very close to tears as well.

Uncle Nick placed something on my chest, and after a while he put his hands on either side of me in a rather hopeless way. There was talk about a drip, and analgesia, and warfarin, and a very poor prognosis.

The Hardest Decision

Mum was crying hopelessly, and Dad could hardly speak. He wanted to take me home to see how I was in the morning, but Uncle Nick didn't think that was a good idea. Mum said something about not letting me suffer. Dad seemed to see the wisdom of that, but fought it emotionally. They might have given me another 24 hours, but perhaps I couldn't have survived that anyway. I just thought, *Please, please, stop this pain and make me better.*

A nurse came into the room and held me while Dad continued to stroke and cuddle me and tickle my chin. Uncle Nick gently lifted my right front paw and snipped away at some of my fur. Then he slipped a needle straight into a vein. I didn't struggle; I was past that. I started to feel sleepy, realised the pain was not as bad, and then there was just...nothing. No pain. Nothing.

I drifted off peacefully to sleep.

Dad's Farewell

Nick explained that Chan had dilated cardiomyopathy: heart failure. Blood must have been collecting in Chan's heart for quite a while because it wasn't being pumped around the body. There it had clotted, and part of the clot had broken off and got stuck in the femoral artery. The lack of effective circulation in the affected leg was the cause of the bluish swelling, and explained why it was colder than the other leg. The prognosis was very, very poor.

It was about half-past ten at night when the last breath left Chan, and he was allowed to fall asleep forever on his side. Nick and the nurse left us for a while.

Then they came back in, confirming gently that our dear friend and companion was dead. They wrapped him in a towel and placed him in the back of our car. It was raining and cold. Somehow, I drove home.

We left Chan in the car overnight. There seemed nowhere else to put him. We each had a stiff drink, and neither slept much that night. And we cried and cried and cried — grown-up sixty-

somethings, both of whom had lost pet animals in the past, crying in so much despair and pain over a cat – but what a cat!

My mother had died a few months earlier, and, sad as that was, neither of us cried over her, and I'm afraid I didn't even feel the need to, despite some feelings of guilt.

Within a few weeks of Chan's death, we would be celebrating our twentieth wedding anniversary. He had been such a large part of our lives for nearly all of those twenty years.

We questioned whether our actions were justified in putting him down to prevent further suffering. We had given him a good life, and he us, and it was such a pity and so sad that it had to end that way – but was there ever going to be a better way?

I had to clear all signs of him away, apart from the photo of him looking out from my computer screensaver. Tins of meat went to the animal shelter from which we had collected him 18 years previously; biscuits went to our neighbour for Dinah. Dishes went into his carrying box.

We went to the boat and removed all signs of him from there, apart from the plaster image that friends had made years before.

Still it rained, and still we cried. Between the storms, with our robin hopping around, we buried Chan in the garden, deep down in the dark, wet earth. We wrapped him not in the vet's towel, but in one of his own: the one we had used in the car to protect the seats from the white fur that he would shed profusely until he got used to travelling.

We laid Chan facing back towards our house, on the track he used so frequently to go to and from our garden and Dinah's. We each gave him a final stroke, and through wet eyes and a chest sore from crying, I covered him over with earth and placed a paving stone on top so that he wouldn't be disturbed by foxes or badgers. We planted at his head a small white rose bush named Special Friend. What other colour or name could we have possibly chosen for him?

And still it rained, and still we cried. It seemed to us that even the world wept.

Chris and Ann Dunn

About Chris and Ann Dunn

Professionally, we – Chris (from Gloucestershire) and Ann (originally from Herefordshire) – are long-time teachers. We both come from families of animal lovers, so there have been numerous occasions when we have lived through, enjoying and experiencing, the life cycles of dearly loved animal family members.

Chan was different, not only because of his unusual markings, but there was also his temperament: warm and cuddly one minute, and the next moment very keen to let us know he had had enough. He made it clear what he wanted or didn't want. In addition, we acquired him (and his friend Charlie) from a local animal shelter not long after we married, when we felt we were ready after the natural death of a previous cat.

All in all, we estimated that he had been with us for around 18 years of our then 20 years of marriage – a special pet, friend, and one of the family.

It took some time to get over his death and go searching for new cats. There could never be a replacement. Our two unrelated black cats are wonderful and different in their individual ways, but there will always be Chan – as this little book has reminded us!

www.ingramcontent.com/pod-product-compliance
Lightning Source LLC
Chambersburg PA
CBHW070551300426
44113CB00011B/1873